This book belongs to:

Natalie was a very popular girl at school.
She always looked nice, brushed her teeth and
brushed her hair. She ate lots of healthy food
and always went to bed early.
She was so cute!

When she started school she was a little shy, but the teachers told her that her hair looked nice.

Lots of children wanted to know where her mother bought the beautiful bobbles that were fancifully attached to her plaits. Everyone at school was friendly and this made Natalie more confident.

Natalie was well behaved at school and did her reading every night. She was good at drawing and liked using vibrant colours in her pictures.

She soon had lots of friends at school! She received invitations to birthday parties and her Mum would meet other parents who told her that they thought she was a delightful girl!

Natalie made friends at church and would go camping with them. She learned skills such as putting up tents, tying knots and the names of stars in the galaxy.

She received her honours badges and was proud of her achievements. Her parents clapped enthusiastically when she received her awards. Her Mummy attached the patches and badges to her forest-green coloured sash.

As Natalie grew into her teenage years, she had an appreciation of how make-up, manicures, pedicures and hairstyling could bring out the best in people's features.

Natalie's Mum introduced her to a salon owner in the city. She was offered work experience for two afternoons a week, she could not wait to get started!

Natalie realised that a session with a good make-up kit made her clients eyes bigger and warmer. Their smiles grew brighter and the new look made them feel better when they gazed at themselves in the mirror.

This was especially important for people when they were attending events such as baby christenings, weddings and graduations.

After finishing secondary school, Natalie attended a local college and studied Hair and Beauty there for two years. She learned how to use the right make up for the different skin tones and how to select good quality products. She also developed an understanding of skin, hair and nail care.

N

Once she was qualified, Natalie had the opportunity to travel as she developed her career.

She managed to get a job with a cruise company. She flew a very long distance from her home to Australia and from there, spent nine months working on a big cruise ship that travelled from Australia to Thailand, Singapore and Malaysia.

In the salon, Natalie worked alongside other beauty therapists to help the people who were on their holidays to look their very best! She met people from around the world and learned about their cultures and heritage.

When she finished her travels, Natalie came back home to work in salons. She helped the people in her home city to look their best.

Salon

Natalie eventually wants to open her own salon in the high street. She hopes to have regular clients who will come to her week after week and she will help them to take care of themselves.

Her clients will appreciate that they must not only look good on the outside but also feel good on the inside. Natalie will remind them to eat the right foods to keep their bodies fit and healthy.

21

She will always take the time to listen to her clients who want to share the things in their lives that make them happy and sad.

So Natalie **is the best beauty therapist**; she cares for her clients in lots of ways!

If you want to be the best beauty therapist, look at these references to learn how!

For Kids:

PBS Kids
Cut colour and style clients hair on this interactive game from PBS Kids!
pbskids.org/peg/games/hair-salon

Toca Boca
Let your kids run their own Toca Hair Salon! Cut, colour, comb, shave and blow-dry lifelike hair on six different cute characters. Using your fingers, you can make just about any hair style you want!
https://tocaboca.com/app/toca-hair-salon/

For parents and guardians:

National Careers Services
National careers service summary of essential aspects of being a beauty therapist, including average salary and working hours.
nationalcareers.service.gov.uk/job-profiles/beauty-therapist

NCC Home Learning
Comprehensive NCC education page on the role of a beauty therapist, career insights and how to join the beauty industry with links to online courses.
www.ncchomelearning.co.uk/how-to-become-a-beauty therapist

UCAS
UCAS guidance on the role of a beauty therapist and the training required to become fully qualified.
www.ucas.com/ucas/after-gcses/find-career-ideas/explore-jobs/job-profile/beauty-therapist

Career Pilot
Career pilot page: job description of beauty consultancy, course entry requirements, employability and career progression.
www.careerpilot.org.uk/job-sectors/beauty-makeup/job-profile/beauty-consultant

What do you want to be when you grow up? Draw it below!

Notes!

Check out some other books in the series!